You Are Loved No Matter What!

A Recovery Devotional

Betty J. Carr

BLACK FOREST PRESS
San Diego, California
July 2000
First Edition

You Are Loved No Matter What!

A Recovery Devotional

Betty J. Carr

PUBLISHED IN THE UNITED STATES OF AMERICA
BY
BLACK FOREST PRESS
P.O.Box 6342
Chula Vista, CA 91909-6342
1-800-451-9404

Books written by Betty J. Carr

The Wisdom of His Word
You are Loved No Matter What

Booklets

Living The Ten Commandments Today
Nuggets From the Throne Room
Spiritual Warfare Prayers
A Garland of Poems
Heralding His Birth

Disclaimer

This document is an original work of the author. It may include reference to information commonly known or freely available to the general public. Any resemblance to other published information is purely coincidental. The author has in no way attempted to use material not of her own origination. Black Forest Press disclaims any association with or responsibility for the ideas, opinions or facts as expressed by the author of this book.

Printed in the United States of America
Library of Congress
Cataloging-in-Publication

ISBN: 1-58275-019-x

Presented to

by

Date

TABLE OF CONTENTS

PART ONE
HAVE YOU BEEN BRUISED?

PART TWO
FORGETTING THE PAST

PART THREE

WHAT DOES GOD SAY?

PART FOUR

ABUSIVE RELATIONSHIPS: DO WE HAVE TO STAY?

PART FIVE

LEARNING TO TRUST AGAIN

PART SIX

OUT OF YOUR SHELL AND ON THE ROAD TO RECOVERY!

ABOUT THE AUTHOR

Betty has traveled the road to recovery, and has been delivered from alcohol, drugs and cigarettes. She knows well the heartache of grief; her husband of 38 years left her for another woman. It is from those deep experiences and the victory over these areas that she addresses others, in the true hope that both men and women will realize that God does love them and that He is their only source of healing.

Betty speaks at churches, retreats, on television and for many women's organizations, including Women AGLOW. She has spoken extensively throughout the United States and Canada. As an ordained minister and author, Betty has helped many individuals going through trials and tribulations to get back on their feet and on the road to recovery. Voted Woman of the Year at the eleventh annual Camarillo Women's Day, for her work with the homeless, Betty is an advocate for those who have been hurt and bruised.

Her first book, *The Wisdom of His Word* is currently a required text for the International College of Bible Theology's course on the Holy Spirit.

Mother of two and grandmother of three, Betty now lives in Southern California with her new husband Bill. He has been a great source of encouragement for this book.

You're Loved No Matter What!

How many of us look for recognition,
self-esteem, and healing from the past?
How many look to "new age", money,
sex, other gods and find they don't last?

There is one though, who truly loves,
forgives, restores and renews.
He shed His blood, so we can all know
how much He loves me and you!

He'll lead you and guide you because
it was for your life He fought
He's been there all along, saying
He loves you, no matter what!

— Betty J. Carr

DEDICATION

To my husband Bill whom God sent to me. He is my faithful companion, husband and friend, who has encouraged me to be all that God has meant me to be. Thank you darling!

ACKNOWLEDGMENTS

To Gail Mallory, Barbara Ausdemore and Kay Swenningsen, who are my faithful prayer partners. Thanks also for your helpful suggestions and your encouragement.

To Anita Bowman of Sunrain Co., San Diego. Thank you for your wonderful cover and illustrations which appear throughout this book.

A WORD FROM THE AUTHOR

The following chapters are for all the hurting people! During my speaking engagements and throughout my ministry, I have been appalled at the number of abused and injured people there are in our society!

I have personally gone through much in my life. This book is a deep sharing of how God can get you through it. He can get you through the hurt and pain and onto the road to recovery. I do not claim to be a doctor, nor do I have any psychiatric training, but I do claim to have found a way out. It is the way out of the hopeless situation many of us have lived or are living in. It is my hope that you will see the truth in the main theme of this book: God loves you no matter what!

B & B Ministries
P O Box 447
Desert Hot Springs, CA
92240
(760) 329-3005 Fax (760) 329- 3225
e-mail: carrbetty@earthlink.net

PREFACE

Why do most of us have trouble believing we are lovable? Why do we search in all the wrong places for love? Why do we have trouble believing our worth?

The enemy goes about as a roaring lion, seeking those whom he can devour! He will use any means — lies, guilt trips, abusive patterns — all making us feel worthless and no good. Many men and women find themselves living in an abusive relationship because they don't feel they deserve better.

But we do. Because God says we do. God says He loves us. He loved us enough to give His Son. And His Son loved us enough to die for us.

"For God so loved the world that He gave His one and only Son, that whoever believes in Him shall not perish but have eternal life. For God did not send His Son into the world to condemn the world, but to save the world through Him."

John 3:16-17

Why else would Satan pull out all the stops in an attempt to make us believe the opposite?

This book will help us deal with the simple and exquisitely wonderful fact that God really does love us. It's not just everyone else He loves, but He also loves YOU.

PART ONE

HAVE YOU BEEN BRUISED?

"He heals the brokenhearted and binds up their wounds."

Psalms 147:3

Why Me?

Be still, and know He is God.
Be still, and rest in Him.
Is it so hard to see
the blessings that surround thee?

It hurts Him to hear
your cries of "why me?"
He lets none endure more then they can,
don't you see?

Instead of thanks
that He's led you out of the night,
instead of thanks
that He's put things right.

He hears your cries
of anguish and despair.
Yet, He tells you,
"I have always been there."

He's never left you,
don't you see?
It was your face
He saw on Calvary.

Dry your tears;
Your burdens, He'll gladly shoulder.
Stand up straight, and know
that from now on you'll be bolder.

Bolder in speaking out
about His truth and way —
a boldness for Him
that will grow each day.

Rest now, little one,
for you have come out of the night.
Never forget, little one
it was all done by His might.

And always remember
how much He loves thee
as He says, "Pick yourself
up and trust in Me!"

— Betty J. Carr

LOW SELF-ESTEEM AND ANXIETY

There are more hurting people out there then we realize. Are you one of those? Many have been hurt by abusive parents. Many have been hurt by taunts from siblings or peers. Many of us have had to overcome years of being told we were stupid or we wouldn't amount to anything. Some of us have been overweight, or some too thin, some slow in learning, or quite intellectual, and some have been traumatically violated. It seems that we all fall into one or another of these categories.

> *"In my anguish, I cried to the LORD, and He answered by setting me free."* **Psalms 118:5**

Let's take a look at some of these wounding forces.

ABUSIVE PARENTS

We must first realize that our fundamental level of self-esteem came from our family. There are many heartbreaking tales of horror at the hands of aggressive, hurtful and cruel parents. Are these parents malicious on purpose or have they themselves been victims of abuse? We can break the cycle of abuse by walking in forgiveness with the help of our Lord, Jesus Christ.

> *"It is mine to avenge; I will repay. In due time their foot will slip; their day of disaster is near and their doom rushes upon them."* **Deuteronomy 32:35**

I am going to hone in on the parent who fails to realize the harm careless words can do. As a child, we have little or no defense against the misplaced allegations that we are no good. The only recourse we have as children is to become angry and belligerent or to become quiet and withdrawn. If our earthly father ignores us or hurts us in any way, is it any wonder we have trouble believing that our heavenly Father loves us no matter what?

"Know therefore that the LORD your God is God; He is the faithful God, keeping His covenant of love to a thousand generations of those who love Him and keep His commands." **Deuteronomy 7:9**

What if our mothers used to tell us we were no good or if our parents seemed to prefer a sister or brother to us? How can we handle this rejection, which generates such profound and painful low self-esteem and creates the expectation that we will be unloved?

My mother used to introduce me as "Betty, my mistake." I cannot tell you how it affected me. I thought somehow I was a mistake who wasn't really supposed to be here on earth. It was only when I turned my heart to Jesus and accepted the fact that He died for me — that I started to be set free. I was released from the terrible path of rejection and low self-esteem that had began as a child and resulted in an abusive marriage as an adult. Even as I received the truth, it took me several years to actually accept that God the Father, as well as Jesus and the Holy Spirit, really loved me.

"You are my refuge and my shield; I have put my hope in your word." **Psalms 119:114**

The harm that can be done with words as well as with physical violence cannot be stressed enough. But the healing of God's word is powerful.

"Do not take revenge, my friends, but leave room for God's wrath, for it is written: "It is mine to avenge; I will repay," says the Lord." **1 Peter 5:7**

One of the ten commandments, "Thou shalt not kill," brings insight and applies to the harm words or verbal abuse can do. Meditate on what you are about to read.

THOU SHALT NOT KILL

"Thou shalt not kill" means more than the physical killing of someone. You can kill someone's spirit, or you can kill with gossip or judgement that causes them such pain, they will believe they can't reach their potential. Or you can kill someone's hopes, aspirations and dreams.

You can kill someone in so many ways. For instance, your child would like to be a fireman, police chief, doctor or lawyer. You tell them "You're stupid." "You won't amount to anything." "You can't do anything right." You kill their basic feelings of self worth. Isn't that killing their hopes, their dreams? You can also kill with kindness, by never correcting or preparing your child to give to others so that they become overbearing and selfish.

And what about your spouse? Do you tell him that he's not making enough money or that he's not a good father? Do you call your wife lazy or tell her she is not a good mother? Don't you think that is also a way of killing a person, beating them down until they have no self-esteem left?

Words are weapons that can scar for life!

Where, then, is the kindness that God gives? What would have happened to you, to us all, if Jesus had done that? Rather, He said, "Be strong and of good courage, fear not."

> *"Be strong and courageous. Do not be afraid or terrified because of them, for the LORD your God goes with you; he will never leave you nor forsake you."* **Deuteronomy 31:6**

God, in his mercy, offers us sonship, throws our sins into the sea of forgetfulness, and sets us free. Can we not extend the same courtesy to others?

"Thou shalt not kill" means many things. Let us search our hearts and ask the Holy Spirit to show us where, under what circumstances, and whom we have killed with our unkind words.

> *"Why do you look at the speck of sawdust in your brother's eye and pay no attention to the plank in your own eye?"* **Matthew 7:3**

Most of us are unaware of the damage our tongues can cause. Let us ask forgiveness from God, and start life anew as we walk the Christian road which our God would have us walk.

"For I am the LORD, your God, who takes hold of your right hand and says to you, Do not fear; I will help you." **Isaiah 41:13**

ABUSED

We are to know from the following scripture that God sees us as the apple of His eye.

"Keep me as the apple of your eye; hide me in the shadow of your wings" **Psalms 17:8**

He desires that we live in freedom from our past mistakes, and freedom from the hurts of our past. We can choose to forgive others; we can choose to forgive ourselves. I cannot stress to you enough that you do have a choice. That is the key. You can choose to accept you are not worth anything. You can choose to believe you don't deserve anything. Or you can choose freedom and Jesus. And those who are free in the Son, Jesus Christ, are free indeed!

Some of us have been so verbally abused, so verbally battered, that we have come to believe that we are lucky if anyone loves us. That is why many of us remain in abusive relationships. Remember, Jesus says otherwise. We have to be healed, and Jesus is the divine Healer. I know. I was an alcoholic, on drugs, smoked three packs of cigarettes a day, and was in an abusive relationship. Since I felt unaccepted as a child, it put me on a path of rejection and low self-esteem. Some of us will try to be as perfect as possible so someone will appreciate us. Others react in the opposite way, becoming destructive and practically defying anyone to love us. But we are all actually the same — broken, hurting individuals, looking for acceptance and love.

Jesus says, "Turn to Me and I will set you free."

"So if the Son sets you free, you will be free indeed." **John 8:36**

Some can receive instant healing; for others, a longer process is required. As with an onion, we get peeled layer by layer until we have total and complete healing. This is the answer to getting over these wrong messages that we believed in error. We have to ask Jesus into our hearts and ask him to turn around those wrong messages we have received.

Since God works good to all those who love Him, He will turn curses into blessings, for nothing is impossible with God.

> *"Jesus looked at them and said, "With man this is impossible, but not with God; all things are possible with God."* **Mark 10:27**

We can learn to trust again by taking the first step and asking Jesus into our hearts, asking the Holy Spirit to take up residence in us.

HURTS FROM OUR SIBLINGS AND PEERS

We have looked at abusive parents as well as the commandment "Thou shalt not kill;" but what defense do we have against our siblings or against the hurts handed to us by our peers? We do have a defense. The defense of choosing not to allow these hurts to color our lives any longer. We can choose to walk in forgiveness.

> *"Then Peter came to Jesus and asked, "Lord, How many times shall I forgive my brother when he sins against me? Up to seven times?" Jesus answered, "I tell you, not seven times, but seventy times seven."* **Matthew 18:21-22**

Walking in forgiveness is a true healing, for it does not heal the person who has hurt us, but it does heal us. If you have not forgiven, then bitterness and resentment can overtake you and start to destroy you. I believe that many illnesses start with this. It is imperative to our health and well-being to walk in forgiveness.

> *"Bear with each other and forgive whatever grievances you may have against one another. Forgive as the Lord forgave you."* **Colossians 3:13**

The Bible says to forgive those who have hurt you. I have counseled with many people who are unable to forgive. They are willing to forgive but the hurt is so intense that they have trouble truly letting go and releasing the feelings they are holding onto. I advise them that to be willing to forgive is sometimes all God asks, and if we invite the Holy Spirit to help us make the forgiveness a reality, it will happen. You see, being willing to forgive is the first step.

Another thing we can do is ask the Lord to show us why such hurtful things were said or done. You will be amazed to find that the perpetrator could have been filled with self-loathing or low self-esteem, trying to prove his or her own self-worth at your expense. You can then have pity for someone like that. You see Jesus loves you no matter what! Only He (if you allow Him) can help you achieve victory over these hurts and slights in your life.

> *"The LORD appeared to us in the past, saying: "I have loved you with an everlasting love; I have drawn you with loving-kindness."* **Jeremiah 31:3**

> *"But God demonstrates His own love for us in this: While we were still sinners, Christ died for us."* **Romans 5:8**

> *"So do not fear, for I am with you; do not be dismayed, for I am your God. I will strengthen you and help you; I will uphold you with My righteous right hand."* **Isaiah 41:10**

OVERWEIGHT OR TOO THIN

We must always bear in mind that the Bible says our bodies are the temple of God.

> *"Do you not know that your body is a temple of the Holy Spirit, who is in you, whom you have received from God? You are not your own; you were bought at a price. Therefore honor God with your body."* **1 Corinthians 6:19-20**

When we invite the Holy Spirit to reside in us, then it is our responsibility to look after this temple. There was a time when I was filled with self-loathing and my body was getting sick. I felt as ill as when I was drinking alcohol and smoking three packs of cigarettes a day. I had developed asthma again, I had gained weight, and I was filled with aches and pains. It was then that I realized I had sinned by not taking care of my temple. And that realization not only brought about deep insight, but an inner healing began to take place. I am now learning to make healthy food choices, as well as "eating to live," not "living to eat."

I am not talking about being overweight or too thin as a child. I do not believe we are held accountable for something that happened to us as children. It is another form of abuse by parents and/or guardians to overfeed or underfeed us. We can pray for balance in our lives and forgive those who made possible the taunts from our siblings or peers. I am speaking now of the Christian who is trying to walk a victorious walk! We have not had enough teaching in our churches about the sin of not looking after the temple of the Holy Spirit, our precious bodies.

> *"If anyone destroys God's temple, God will destroy him; for God's temple is sacred, and you are that temple."* **1 Corinthians 3:17**

The important thing to remember is that we have a choice in how we react and in how we view our situation. How did I get over being called a mistake? I realized that my mother meant no harm. You see, I was a "change of life" baby and she was embarrassed at being a new mother at the age of 45. So, I chose to take the hurtful words out of the air, by substituting them with "This is Betty, my blessing." I cannot tell you how much this "repatterning" has helped me and the healing it has brought. You, too, can have the same kind of victory if you do this.

> *"No, in all these things we are more than conquerors through Him who loved us."*
> **Romans 8:37**

VIOLATED

Often the person who is violated is made to feel that it is somehow their fault. Anyone who perpetrates abuse to someone else's body is operating under the orders of Satan. Yet, Satan doesn't stop there. He then tells his victim that they are dirty, that no one would ever want them, or that sex is dirty. As a result, many victims become either frigid or promiscuous. How do we get over this type of abuse and become compassionate, kind, beloved and well-balanced people?

> *"Therefore, as God's chosen people, holy and dearly loved, clothe yourselves with compassion, kindness, humility, gentleness and patience. Bear with each other and forgive whatever grievances you may have against one another. Forgive as the Lord forgave you. And over all these virtues put on love, which binds them all together in perfect unity."* **Colossians 3:12-14**

It is once again the choice to walk in forgiveness. Understand that you were not at fault. Chances are you were just a child. Read the Song of Solomon in the Bible. God meant sex to be the fulfillment of love — not to be used abusively, but with tenderness. He made man and woman to walk side by side and to be joined together. If you understand that the perpetrator is sick, it will help, and remember — the bitterness, resentment, and unforgiveness coming from these experiences will make you sick, not the one who hurt you. I have counseled many men and women who all get a tremendous emotional and spiritual release when they choose to forgive and realize that they were not at fault. I have many speaking engagements and it never ceases to amaze me that, on the average, 80% of the audience have been violated or abused. It is time to get a healing. If you turn to Jesus, our Divine Healer, He will set you free of the agony you carry with you.

> *"The LORD is close to the brokenhearted and saves those who are crushed in spirit."*
> **Psalms 34:18**

Turn to part 6, "Out of Your Shell and Onto the Road of Victory," for more insights into all of these topics.

> *"Though I walk in the midst of trouble, You preserve my life; you stretch out Your hand against the anger of my foes, with Your right hand You save me."* **Psalms 138:7**

> *"Peace I leave with you; my peace I give you. I do not give to you as the world gives. Do not let your hearts be troubled and do not be afraid."* **John 14:27**

RESULTS FROM NEGATIVE CHILDHOOD MESSAGES

When we as children have received the negative messages profiled in the previous outlines, we find that unless we deal with these thoughts and feelings, they can rule our lives. The residue can shape our decision-making without our even realizing it.

What decisions?

- You came from an abusive family . . . you marry an abuser.
- You believe you would never amount to anything . . .you take a job that sets you up for failure or verbal abuse.
- You find you are angry at anyone and everyone, including God…you feed yourself hatred.
- Your attitudes are all wrong…you set yourself up for failure and heartbreak.
- You were ravished, so you overeat to become unattractive to the opposite sex…You think you are protecting yourself, for nobody would want you looking like this.

You are not an awful person because you have reacted in any of the above ways. Understanding why you have made wrong decisions is the beginning of healing.

> *"Cast your cares on the LORD and he will sustain you; he will never let the righteous fall."* **Psalms 55:22**

What can you do?

1. Understand that although you don't feel it at times, God does love you.
2. Imagine putting the perpetrator in a chair, and venting your anger, even to hitting them in order to get closure to the situation and a forgiving heart.
3. You may need counseling. If so, get a Christian counselor who is well versed in the Bible.
4. Read this book over and over until you have it in your spirit.

All is not lost. God does love you. You can be healed. When the reason for your low self-esteem or destructive behavior patterns is brought to light, then the healing process can start.

> *"Then maidens will dance and be glad, young men and old as well. I will turn their mourning into gladness; I will give them comfort and joy instead of sorrow."* **Jeremiah 31:13**

PRAYER FOR HEALING OF MEMORIES

There is a way of praying for the healing of past experiences. It is sometimes called "The Healing of Memories," sometimes "Psychological Healing." It rests on the fact that Jesus is the Lord of all time; past, present, and future, that He can even change the past.

"Lord Jesus, I ask you now to walk into my subconscious mind and heal the wounds of my inner child — the unloved child, the abandoned child, the abused child, and heal all the wounds of my childhood. Thank you Lord, for healing the wounds of my soul — the scars resulting from my own deliberate sins in thought, word, and deed. Cleanse and make me whole. Set me free Lord Jesus from all unforgiveness, bitterness and hatred. Let your divine love and peace flood my soul. In your mercy Lord Jesus bring healing to my body. Keep me faithful to your Love and steadfast in the daily tribulations of life. Let your perfect Will be fulfilled in me. Thank you Lord Jesus, my Shepherd and Divine Physician."

— with permission of Father Pat Crowley

NOTES AND PRAYERS

PART TWO

FORGETTING THE PAST

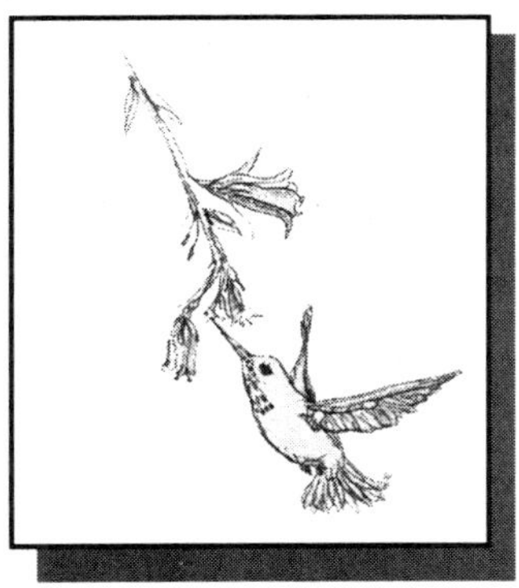

"Be strong and courageous. Do not be afraid or terrified because of them, for the LORD your God goes with you; he will never leave you nor forsake you."
Deuteronomy. 31:6

The Greater Plan

God sees your sorrows.
Was not His son crucified?
Look to Him. He is the Lord that healeth.

Give Him your heart: He will wash
away your tears. Have faith;
He did not lift you up to fall.
Hold out your hand: He will give you
the peace that passeth all understanding.

Look to God's word: He is the "I Am."
He loves you and asks you to put out your hand.
He will lead you out of the darkness
into peace and tranquility.

God loves you. Give Him all your burdens;
Know He sees the greater plan.
Put your trust in Him.
He is the Lord God.

— Betty J. Carr

INTRODUCTION

Some of us have received wrong messages all our lives. They have been messages that tell us that we are no good, messages that tell us we will fail no matter how hard we try, or we get messages that we are unlovable. We have to take care not to entertain these thoughts and believe them for they are destructive. These messages are not from God. We must understand that God's word and His love for us can dispel all the negative, destructive statements and change them into positive, life-giving thoughts.

> *"The tongue that brings healing is a tree of life, but a deceitful tongue crushes the spirit."* **Proverbs 15:4**

> *"The salvation of the righteous comes from the LORD; He is their stronghold in time of trouble. The LORD helps them and delivers them; He delivers them from the wicked and saves them, because they take refuge in Him."* **Psalms 37:39-40**

Let's take a look at this, shall we?

PRIDE

Is it possible that one main cause of our accepting these wrong messages is pride?

> *"Pride goes before destruction, a haughty spirit before a fall."* **Proverbs 16:18**

Pride can get an insidious hold on anyone who does not walk in meekness and humility! It can come from low self-esteem, rejection or as a response to fear. Here's how this can happen.

LIFESTYLES

In the beginning of the church, people gave up their personal possessions and combined what they had, thus defeating individual pride. I am merely pointing this out, for this, of course, is not the only way.

> *"A greedy man stirs up dissension, but he who trusts in the LORD will prosper. He who trusts in himself is a fool, but he who walks in wisdom is kept safe."* **Proverbs 28:25-26**

Please realize that neither having nor lacking money will make you better or worse than anyone else. Each person has his or her given walk, given purpose, given destiny to fulfill. If you walk in pride, how can you fulfill anything but your own desires and wishes? When you do that you'll find you are living an unfulfilled life.

LOW SELF-ESTEEM

Why do you feel less than someone else? Why do you reject walking in God's healing and in the fullness of life He offers?

> *"So do not fear, for I am with you; do not be dismayed, for I am your God. I will strengthen you and help you; I will uphold you with My righteous right hand."* **Isaiah 41:10**

Rejection and low self-esteem are actually another aspect of pride. God's word says that He knew us in our mother's womb. He also says that He is Jehovah Raphe, our healer. Since that is true, you must examine your heart. God often allows pain in your life to help you grow. Are you so special, so prideful that you are somehow above learning the lessons your Father is giving you? Instead say, "Since You knew me in my mother's womb, and You are the healer, I ask you, Lord, to remove the scars of my past. Please correct any wrong messages I have received about being less than others or not wanted. I trust You to heal me." By saying this you are letting go of your pride.

> *Though the LORD is on high, he looks upon the lowly, but the proud he knows from afar.*
> **Psalms 138:6**

He heals the brokenhearted and binds up their wounds. **Psalms 147:3**

"But He was pierced for our transgressions, He was crushed for our iniquities; the punishment that brought us peace was upon Him, and by His wounds we are healed." **Isaiah 53:5**

FEAR

Have you ever told yourself, "Everyone is looking at me. Therefore, I can't make a mistake or I'll look foolish." Or perhaps you've had many costly possessions, and now have to down scale and it's embarrassing. These thoughts are all prideful, for you are more concerned with what people think, than what God thinks.

"For God did not give us a spirit of timidity, but a spirit of power, of love and of self-discipline." **2 Timothy 1:7**

Pride can get hold of you in the most seemingly innocent way. Perhaps you say, "I want what God wants in my life," but in reality, you are secretly afraid of making a mistake.

If you learn to turn all cares, all concerns over to the Holy Spirit, only then can He take away your fear, your low self-esteem and feelings of rejection.

"God is our refuge and strength, an ever-present help in trouble." **Psalms 46:1**

And the peace of God, which transcends all understanding, will guard your hearts and your minds in Christ Jesus. **Philippians 4:7**

We have reviewed pride and lifestyles, pride and low self esteem along with pride and fear. Check yourself in these areas, get right before God and in the process receive spiritual healing.

TURNING ALL TO GOOD

I have found that another way to get over hurtful messages is to ask the Lord to turn it to good. In other words, ask Him to let you help others who are going through trials similar to what you have been through.

> *"And we know that in all things God works for the good of those who love Him, who have been called according to His purpose."* **Romans 8:28**

I am a living example of this. I started working with the homeless. These were people who needed food and comfort.

> *"For He will deliver the needy who cry out, the afflicted who have no one to help. He will take pity on the weak and the needy and save the needy from death."* **Psalms 72:12-13**

The Lord had a plan for my life. My church, along with 28 other churches of various denominations, joined together to rent a building that had a kitchen and large eating hall to feed those in need. My church, although I was still just a babe in Christ, put me in charge of our church's feeding program. I was inspired to play soft music, and before we opened the doors we walked around the hall and prayed for the blood of Jesus to bless and help those who came. We had thirteen regular servers and sixty men and women who took turns cooking the meals. Our church provided the cooks with a recipe and all the ingredients along with a baking pan. This was available for them after Sunday service. They would then return it to church early the next morning. This worked well since we served on Mondays. We did it this way so that the burden of providing the ingredients, as well as the cooking, didn't fall to the usual workers in our church. In this way, no one had to miss a blessing of helping God's poor, if they themselves couldn't afford the ingredients; it also helped keep people from having "burn-out." With sixty cooks, each only had to cook once every four months, and everyone in our church wanted to be a part of it. It was called "Family to Family."

I loved it, for the Lord had seared my heart for the less fortunate. It was during one of these meals while I was walking around the hall seeing that everyone was served, that it was laid on my heart to "Share." Share? Me? In obedience, I stood up on an elevated stairwell and told those present that I was a recovered alcoholic, a heavy smoker, and addicted to Valium. I shared that I had asked Jesus to help me get sober and well again. He was faithful and gave me strength to face my addictions, one day at a time. At the time, along with severe withdrawals, my body was thrown into a pit of despair, a pit so black that even suicide seemed welcome. Only the knowledge of the fact that Jesus was with me could I stay on the path to sobriety.

> *"He gives strength to the weary and increases the power of the weak."* **Isaiah 40:29**

To my surprise, most of the people there knew what I was talking about. They had been viewing all of us as prissy Christians, not understanding what any of them were going through. Yet, when in obedience, I shared what the Lord had done in my life, hundreds came to the Lord.

Seeing lives changed so dramatically made every bit of pain and suffering I had gone through worthwhile.

> *"Your people settled in it, and from your bounty, O God, you provided for the poor."* **Psalms 68:10**

You, too, can ask the Lord to use you to help others, thus turning those wrong messages into messages of hope. I want to encourage you that God does not show partiality. What He has done for me, He can do for you and more!

> *"Do not show partiality in judging; hear both small and great alike. Do not be afraid of any man, for judgment belongs to God. Bring Me any case too hard for you, and I will hear it."* **Deuteronomy 1:17**

> *"So do not fear, for I am with you; do not be dismayed, for I am your God. I will strengthen you and help you; I will uphold you with My righteous right hand."* **Isaiah 41:10**

UNDERSTANDING GOD'S LOVE FOR YOU

There are, of course, other ways to get over the past; you have just read about two of them. Another way to be released from the past is to simply understand how much Jesus loves you. The Bible says that God knew us before we were born.

> *"Yet You brought me out of the womb; You made me trust in You even at my mother's breast. From birth I was cast upon You; from my mother's womb You have been my God."* **Psalms 22:9-10**

Since that is so, does it not stand to reason that He has a purpose for your life? Whether you are used in helping others overcome the same problems that you have had or wanting to become a better parent, teacher, child, person, the important thing is, know and understand how much God loves you. If you will take the time to read and meditate on the scriptures that have been given to you in love, in order to validate and qualify what is being said, it will bring about healing. Holding onto the truth of how much you are loved, will definitely help you on the road to recovery, as well as lead you to a healing.

Understanding how much you are loved will erase the wrong messages of the past and put positive messages into your spirit, soul and body.

> *"And the LORD said, "I will cause all my goodness to pass in front of you, and I will proclaim My name, the LORD, in your presence. I will have mercy on whom I will have mercy, and I will have compassion on whom I will have compassion."* **Exodus 33:19**

> *"Then my enemies will turn back when I call for help. By this I will know that God is for me."* **Psalms 56:9**

REPLAYING THE PAST

Another way of getting over the past is by replaying it and "repatterning" it. Remember back in Chapter One when I had replaced the words, "This is Betty, my mistake," with "This is Betty, my blessing." You too can use this method to get over hurtful messages.

> *"If you then, though you are evil, know how to give good gifts to your children, how much more will your Father in heaven give the Holy Spirit to those who ask Him!"* **Luke 11:13**

Just remember that it was not God who said you were no good. It was not God who said you wouldn't amount to anything. It was not God who said you were unlovable. No, on the contrary, He said He formed you in your mother's womb. He said He gave you a sound mind.

> *"This is what the LORD says — your Redeemer, who formed you in the womb: I am the LORD, who has made all things, who alone stretched out the heavens, who spread out the earth by myself"* **Isaiah 44:24**

> *"This is what the LORD says — He who made you, who formed you in the womb, and who will help you: Do not be afraid, O Jacob, my servant, Jeshurun, whom I have chosen."* **Isaiah 44:2**

He has chosen you. He promises to be your refuge, your port in time of trouble. Hold onto that promise and ask the Holy Spirit to make these words, the Word of God, real and alive to you.

And He will.

> *"Keep me safe, O God, for in You I take refuge."* **Psalms 16:1**

PRAYER FOR HEALING OF EMOTIONS

> *"But during the night an angel of the Lord opened the doors of the jail and brought them out. "Go, stand in the temple courts," he said, "and tell the people the full message of this new life."* **Acts 5:19-20**

"Lord, I have been kept a prisoner by my remembrances as well as my emotions. Send your holy angel to open "my" prison doors I pray. Lead me out of the dark and into your light. May I become all you would have me to be."

— Betty J. Carr

NOTES AND PRAYERS

God's Path!

My child, walk beside Me
night and day.
In all you do,
ask for direction and pray.

I have been merciful
just and kind.
I kept you protected,
for you are Mine.

So, even though
this trial seems severe.
Hold to the promise
that I am always near.

When victory comes
at the end of this test,
remember, I told you
that I knew best.

For it took you,
yourself to lay flesh down,
for the victory trumpet
to start to sound.

Always remember this time
of trial and error.
Remember My child,
that My path is always better.

So listen for My low voice
that says, "No, not that path.
This is the one; ah,
you're safe at last."

— Betty J. Carr

PART THREE

WHAT DOES GOD SAY?

"The righteous cry out, and the LORD hears them; He delivers them from all their troubles."
PSALMS 34:17

INTRODUCTION

Our Lord never promised us a life without tribulation. Rather, He said there would indeed be many trials and tribulations in our lives. He also, however, allows us freedom of choice. This fundamental freedom is what I would like to address.

> *"The LORD is good, a refuge in times of trouble. He cares for those who trust in Him."* **Nahum 1:7**

DOORS OF CHOICE

> *This is what the LORD says: "Stand at the crossroads and look; ask for the ancient paths, ask where the good way is, and walk in it, and you will find rest for your souls. But you said, 'We will not walk in it.'"* **Jeremiah 6:16**

Since we are allowed free choice, we usually have more than one way to go, more than one door that we can choose to walk through. The Lord would have us know that if one door opens, there is always another door we can walk through. These doors are called "Life's Choices." Sometimes if you walk through a door, it is a door of convenience; other doors are a passageway through your fears.

> *"For God did not give us a spirit of timidity, but a spirit of power, of love and of self-discipline."*
> **2 Timothy 1:7**

If you go through this kind of door, you come face to face with your fear, thereby putting it to light and permitting the truth to set you free. But if you choose a door of convenience, it is usually one where you can hide your head, thereby not facing the fear. You see, Jesus' apostles were met with these doors and choices all the time. They chose the doors of exhortation, of confrontation, if these would lead to God's glory.

> *"Judas and Silas, who themselves were prophets, said much to encourage and strengthen the brothers."* **Acts 15:32**

"Brothers, I urge you to bear with My word of exhortation, for I have written you only a short letter." **Hebrews 13:22**

Some of us may choose to ignore the correct door. We keep looking for the door of convenience. Then the Lord must force us to go through the correct door and find the passageway through our fears. By trying to avoid the truth and facing the inevitable, we endure many negative things longer than need be. When we have the courage to walk through the right door, we will find that we have achieved freedom and peace.

"For this God is our God forever and ever; He will be our guide even to the end." **Psalms 48:14**

Some of us may choose the door of man rather than of God; we have to endure more than we would, had we chosen the correct door in the first place. Some of us may choose doors of convenience, and some, unwisely, doors of destruction. If only we could have had the courage to examine all of our choices from front to back and back to front. If only we would take the time to check our choice against the Word of God, as well as seek the Lord's guidance in prayer, we would be much happier and less distraught.

"If the LORD delights in a man's way, He makes His steps firm" **Psalms. 37:23**

This scripture pertains to most of life's decisions, but in particular to the important decisions that could deeply affect our lives.

"If any of you lacks wisdom, he should ask God, who gives generously to all without finding fault, and it will be given to him. But when he asks, he must believe and not doubt, because he who doubts is like a wave of the sea, blown and tossed by the wind." **James 1:5-6**

I can remember a time when I felt so full of despair, so unloved and unlovable, that I actually decided to drink. That's right, I decided that if I drank I could handle things much better. In defense of myself, however, I never even realized that

I had a choice. I never dreamt that I could choose not to live in fear any longer — that I could choose not to undergo constant verbal abuse day in and day out. Some of us get so down-trodden that we either don't realize that we have a choice or we were never taught that we had a choice.

Our heavenly Father, who loves us so much, gives us a choice. In His infinite wisdom He gave us free will. We can choose to walk away from Him or walk to Him. It is our choice.

Yet, there is the greatest freedom in walking to Him. He will kiss away all of our tears and will take all our fears from us. He will set our feet on a firm path. I always claim that Psalms 40:2 is the story of my life.

> *"He lifted me out of the slimy pit, out of the mud and mire; He set my feet on a rock and gave me a firm place to stand."* **Psalms 40:2**

I chose to call out to Jesus! And the most amazing point is this: no matter what I had done, Jesus welcomed me back with open arms.

> *"If we confess our sins, He is faithful and just and will forgive us our sins and purify us from all unrighteousness. If we claim we have not sinned, we make Him out to be a liar and His word has no place in our lives."* **1 John 1:9-10**

I had walked so far from Him, and yet the very moment I called out to him my soul was flooded with a great peace. I clung to Jesus as I walked through the rough road that is the process of sobriety. Each day I grew more and more accustomed to feeling my strength return. I had many issues in my life to get straight, but I took it slow and walked one day at a time, putting all my trust in Him.

Believe me when I tell you He will never fail you! What He has done for me, He can do for you.

Because He loves you — no matter what!

STEPS TO GOOD DECISION-MAKING

There are many scriptures that give us direction for our daily walk. However, I have condensed a few steps that will help us make Godly decisions for our lives.

"I will instruct you and teach you in the way you should go; I will counsel you and watch over you." **Psalms 32:8**

Ask yourself these questions:

1. Am I obedient or disobedient to God's word?
2. Is the door I am about to enter, a door of convenience, or will it take me through my fear?
3. Am I ignoring the situation or am I confronting my fear?
4. Is my heart right? Am I thinking clearly and without prejudice?
5. Will my decision bring guilt or serenity?
6. Do I feel confusion or peace about my decision?
7. Is it wise financially or not?
8. Is it good for my health?

"Do not conform any longer to the pattern of this world, but be transformed by the renewing of your mind. Then you will be able to test and approve what God's will is — His good, pleasing and perfect will." **Romans 12:2**

"It is because of Him that you are in Christ Jesus, who has become for us wisdom from God — that is, our righteousness, holiness and redemption." **1 Corinthians 1:30**

If we ask ourselves these questions and, of course, if we also sincerely ask for God's guidance, how can we choose the wrong door? However, if we do get off track, we must remember our God is merciful and kind. He allows us to choose our own doors, but if we choose the wrong door, praise God, He has mercy on us. And if we cry for help, He will lead us back to the right door; the door to healing and freedom.

"Trust in the LORD with all your heart and lean not on your own understanding; In all your ways acknowledge Him, and He will make your paths straight." **Proverbs 3:5-6**

When You Pray!

If you could learn, when you pray
"Lord, help me do Your will today."
Can you not see the freeing that would bring,
and at the same time, bring glory to the King?

If you could learn, each day
to lay your pride down and say
"Not my will, but Yours be done."
You will bring glory to the Son.

If you learn to start each day,
asking "Holy Spirit help me pray.
May I be a light in this world for You."
Think of the good that you could do.

For it is not in your strength you stand,
for I am the one holding your hand.
So let your heart and your soul sing,
"Glory to God, His Spirit and Jesus our King."

— Betty J. Carr

NOTES AND PRAYERS

Destruction!

The path of destruction is very wide;
it beckons to each who will hear;
it entices and draws you close to death,
but remember, I, your Lord, am near.

Have I not promised to all of you
who wish to please and love Me so,
that I will lift you out of destruction's path,
for I will tell you which way to go.

Oh, My children, if you could be
aware of the traps and snares,
if you could only understand
to avoid them, takes prayer.

For the evil one seeks whom he can devour
taking joy in your tears.
Yet, I tell you, I have defeated him
and you are to remember I am near.

So stand up once again My child,
stand up and know,
when you reach the crossroads in life,
I will show you which way to go.

— Betty J. Carr

PART FOUR

ABUSIVE RELATIONSHIPS: DO WE HAVE TO STAY?

"If anyone does not provide for his relatives,
and especially for his immediate family,
he has denied the faith and is worse than an unbeliever."
1 Timothy 5:8

DO WE HAVE TO STAY?

If we find ourselves in an abusive relationship, it is because most of us do not feel we deserve any better. The abuser usually asserts power over the abused with fear. We become afraid of many things — of retaliation, of being abandoned, afraid of being physically hurt, afraid of never finding another to put up with us. We can also become afraid of other people, of being rejected again, afraid of the future, afraid of being "found out." We become so accustomed to living in fear, that it becomes familiar to us.

> *"There is no fear in love. But perfect love drives out fear, because fear has to do with punishment. The one who fears is not made perfect in love."*
> **1 John 4:18**

Some abusers rule us with money.

> *"Keep your lives free from the love of money and be content with what you have, because God has said, "Never will I leave you; never will I forsake you."* **Hebrews 13:5**

Because we can't afford to live without them, we continue to accept abuse. This pertains in particular to women. Although we live in a modern society, it is still a woman's nature to nurture and look after her children. Many times the man or husband makes a larger salary, so a woman fears she could not survive financially and look after her children if she were to leave him. But look at what God says:

> *"If that is how God clothes the grass of the field, which is here today, and tomorrow is thrown into the fire, how much more will he clothe you, O you of little faith!"* **Luke 12:28**

Now let's look at the other side of this: what harm is she doing to her children, as well as herself, if she stays? God never intended us to be doormats. When He says to us to turn the other cheek, I believe He means to give someone the benefit of the doubt. However, if you are married to a verbal or physical abuser, I believe you have to leave for survival. Remember what God says about this in Part Three, "What does God say?"

> *"It is for freedom that Christ has set us free. Stand firm, then, and do not let yourselves be burdened again by a yoke of slavery."* **Galatians 5:1**

EXAMPLE

I am a prime example of living in an abusive relationship. As I mentioned, my mother, calling me a "mistake," set me on a path of low self-esteem and self-loathing. I lived in fear almost all my life; fear that I was not supposed to be here on earth, fear that my mother would leave me, fear that if I wasn't good enough in school or any other thing I attempted, that people wouldn't like me, and then later, in fear of my husband. You see, patterns get established in our lives. We must become aware of these, so we can break destructive habit patterns. When my husband of 38 years left me for another woman, it was the ultimate in rejection, the fulfillment of my worst fears.

> *"Those who know your name will trust in you, for you, LORD, have never forsaken those who seek you."* **Psalms 9:10**

I felt like a failure. I felt abandoned. I felt unloved. I felt disgraced. And I felt that since I was so unlovable I would live alone all my life. NOT SO! God didn't tell me I was a failure. God didn't abandon me. God didn't tell me He didn't love me. God knew I did the best I could to be a good wife. And finally, God did not reject me.

> *"Even though I walk through the valley of the shadow of death, I will fear no evil, for You are with me; Your rod and your staff, they comfort me. You prepare a table before me in the presence of my enemies. You anoint my head with oil; my cup overflows."* **Psalms 23:4-5**

One of the things we must remember and get into our hearts is this: we cannot look to man for fulfillment or acceptance, because we will meet with failure and disappointment frequently. Rather, look to God. In Him we will receive healing and fulfillment.

You must allow yourself time to grieve, and time to get over the deep hurt and rejection. Although it is painful, if you have Jesus, then you have the only source of real comfort.

By the way, God has brought me a new husband. One who loves the Lord, who is kind and gentle with me, one who encourages me. I have never been happier.

> *"No longer will they call you Deserted, or name your land Desolate. But you will be called Hephzibah, and your land Beulah; for the LORD will take delight in you, and your land will be married."* **Isaiah 62:4**

I do not recommend divorce or separation to anyone. It is a painful process similar to, or worse than a death. However, let's look at some options.

OPTIONS

We usually have two doors of choice which we may walk through. One door is usually the passageway through our fears, and the other door is the convenient way. Suppose you are thinking of leaving your husband or wife. (I am not talking divorce, but separation).

Ask yourself these questions:

1. Would I be safer?
2. What would happen to me if I left? (It is not God's will that you stay in an abusive relationship.)
3. Where will I live?
4. If I don't have enough money, what kind of job can I get?

Next, look at the variables in the other door.

1. Do I have Biblical reasons for working on this marriage?
2. Is this what God would have me do?

3. Can I rekindle our love; and if I have lost respect or love for him/her, can it be restored?
4. Can I change myself to help this situation?
5. Would counseling help; and if he/she wouldn't go, then would it help me?

Now you may also be in the midst of the situation and unable to see clearly. I went to a Christian recovery program at a church. The benefits were enormous, for I learned I was not alone, there were other women in my shoes and I found that the men in the program had been as devastated as the women had been. You see we were all hurting individuals.

> *"If anyone does not provide for his relatives, and especially for his immediate family, he has denied the faith and is worse than an unbeliever."*
> **1 Timothy 5:8**

> *"Persecuted, but not abandoned; struck down, but not destroyed."* **2 Corinthians 4:9**

Then there is the heartbreak you face when the unbelieving spouse leaves you. You must face the fact that you are not a failure and you have not been abandoned by God. God loves you no matter what! You must also face the fact that God's word says to let the unbeliever go.

> *"But if the unbeliever leaves, let him do so. A believing man or woman is not bound in such circumstances; God has called us to live in peace."* **1 Corinthians 7:15**

See what happens when you take a problem or a decision and explore it fully? There may even be a time when you have to wait on the Lord to help you see all the sides of the issue, but God is faithful. Does He not promise in James 1:5 to guide and direct us?

> *"If any of you lacks wisdom, he should ask God, who gives generously to all without finding fault, and it will be given to him."* **James 1:5**

When you are struggling to reach a decision, make sure you are not in disobedience to God's word. Have faith and trust that the answer will come, and it will.

Jesus' apostles were met with these doors of decision and choices all the time. They chose the door of exhortation and of confrontation, if it would lead to His glory.

> *"And let us consider how we may spur one another on toward love and good deeds."* **Hebrews. 10:24**

> *"If it is encouraging, let him encourage; if it is contributing to the needs of others, let him give generously; if it is leadership, let him govern diligently; if it is showing mercy, let him do it cheerfully."* **Romans 12:8**

PRAYER OF FORGIVENESS

"Father, I lift to you my tarnished body and mind darkened with sin.

"I ask you for forgiveness on bended knee. Wash me in your blood I pray, cleanse me and make me whole. Put me once again on your holy highway. Indwell me with such intensity that I cannot, nor will I desire to stray from you. Hold me I pray, as a Father holds his child, protected in his arms.

"Keep me safe in the palm of your hand and then, I pray embolden me to speak your truth. Empower me to set the prisons free. Guide and lead me to help others in the way everlasting."

—Betty J. Carr

NOTES AND PRAYERS

PART FIVE

LEARNING TO TRUST AGAIN

"Trust in the LORD with all your heart and lean not on your own understanding; in all your ways acknowledge Him, and He will make your paths straight."
Proverbs. 3:5-6

Why Be Downcast?

Why be downcast, oh my soul?
For I have the Lord's love to make me whole.
Why look at circumstances with eyes of despair?
When I can look to the Lord and know He cares.

Oh for the lies of this world to end.
Oh for our Kings return, and then
paradise, so wonderful and sweet,
and the Lord of Lords, at last I'll meet.

— Betty J. Carr

HOW CAN WE LEARN TO TRUST AGAIN?

Why should we trust again? Many have been hurt to the quick, battered and bruised in ego, often putting up walls within their hearts so they will not be hurt again. These walls protect them, so they think. But the walls stop people from reaching them and closes their ears to God's voice telling them that they are loved — that they are okay!

> *"For you are a people holy to the LORD your God. The LORD your God has chosen you out of all the peoples on the face of the earth to be his people, his treasured possession."* **Deuteronomy. 7:6**

Only the Holy Spirit working in our hearts can help us to truly open our hearts to receive healing.

If we can just say the sinner's prayer on page 53, and renew our dedication to the Lord, we can start on the road to recovery.

TRUSTING AGAIN

A lot of people say, "How can I trust again?" "I won't allow anyone to hurt me like that again." I can say through my own experience, it takes time to heal. Hold unto Jesus because He will not desert you! You may go through many feelings — anger, frustration, even hatred. Yet if you ask the Holy Spirit to give you a heart of forgiveness, which is what I did, then this healing process will be immeasurably shorter.

> *"Blessed are those who are persecuted because of righteousness, for theirs is the kingdom of heaven. Blessed are you when people insult you, persecute you and falsely say all kinds of evil against you because of me. Rejoice and be glad, because great is your reward in heaven, for in the same way they persecuted the prophets who were before you."* **Matthew 5:10-12**

If you, like me, prayed every day for your spouse, stood on the promise of a healed relationship along with a spouse who would be kind to you, and he still left, I suggest you had better check your heart to see if you are trying to blame Jesus. I know I was angry with God. I didn't understand how He could have allowed this to happen. However, we are not robots, but have choices. God will do all He can to preserve a marriage but if the spouse chooses to leave, we must let him go and not blame God. If your spouse abuses you physically or verbally and you continue to pray for him yet he chooses not to change, then you need to seek God on what you are to do. Maybe a separation is needed.

We must really believe that since He loves you and died for you, then why would He try to hurt you or make you miserable? Even in this situation, you have to believe that something better will come through this; that God intends a blessing and not a curse. When you are hurt and wounded, only God can help you to trust again.

> *"Do not be overcome by evil, but overcome evil with good."* **Romans 12:21**

You see, the disbelief, the hurt, and the tide of remorse and then anger when your spouse tells you he is not happy with you any more and he wants a divorce, can almost kill you. I remember crying my eyes out, as if my heart would break. Yet, somewhere inside me, I knew that if I harbored resentment, that I would be the one who got sick. So even then, I prayed, "Father please forgive them. Help me to forgive them and hold it not against them."

> *"For it is commendable if a man bears up under the pain of unjust suffering because he is conscious of God. But how is it to your credit if you receive a beating for doing wrong and endure it? But if you suffer for doing good and you endure it, this is commendable before God. To this you were called, because Christ suffered for you, leaving you an example, that you should follow in his steps. He committed no sin, and no deceit was found in his mouth. When they hurled their insults at him, he did not retaliate; when he suffered, he made no threats. Instead, he entrusted himself to him who judges justly."* **1 Peter 2:19-23**

I healed very quickly because of that prayer. I know each person's situation is different but I believe the solution is the same for all of us. We all must walk in forgiveness.

In Part Three, we took a more in-depth look at the sections, "Doors of Choice" and "The Steps To Good Decision-Making."

MEMORIES

Thoughts brought to remembrance can be either destructive or constructive. Destructive ones lead you away from the Lord, and constructive ones lead you to Him. When your memories flood in, they can be used for either healing or injury (to you). Memories can be clouded with "should haves" or "I wish." Take each memory, exactly as it is, and deal with it. Do not let it deal with you.

Destructive memories can generate many negative reactions:

1. Unforgiveness: giving in to a desire for either self-pity or revenge.
2. Sadness: looking at what could have been, whipping yourself for what you did not do, feelings of loneliness.
3. Physical stress: can lead to ill health with ailments such as, stomach problems, heart palpitations, or high blood pressure.
4. Avoidance: destructive memories can lead to a running away, rather then facing a memory or circumstances too painful to face.

Constructive memories can lead to:

1. Forgiveness: if you were in an abusive relationship, whether with parents, siblings, or a spouse, they can help you see clearly whether or not you were truly at fault in any way. You can then ask God for forgiveness, and forgive yourself. If you find that you were not at fault and you were shabbily treated, again forgive. Your willingness to check your own heart is the key.

2. Healing: if you have asked for forgiveness, then your heart will be healed, as well as physical ailments that stem from deep bitterness.
3. Happiness: constructive memories can lead to a light heartedness and a freeing as never before.

Memories serve many purposes, and it is up to you to make the right choice. Will you have them destructive or constructive? The lesson here is to deal with them, put them in their proper perspective. If you truly do this, the memories that haunt you will become just that—memories that cannot hurt you, nor touch you anymore.

If the memory is pleasant then remember it with joy, but do not dwell on it, for yesterday as well as tomorrow will look after itself. You must live in today.

Constructive memories are also a way of walking in today, not yesterday. You receive a healing from the past by looking at a memory from all sides. You can either repent or forgive, thus enabling you to put the memory aside and consider it resolved. To walk in today, which is another way of walking in faith and freedom, requires putting memories to rest. When you walk in today, you meet each circumstance or tribulation by looking at it head on. When you walk in today, you do not project worry about the future or into a situation, but you instead look at every challenge by saying, "Lord, what would bring you glory today?" or "What would Jesus do?" or "What is your will for me today"?

You see, this is a process. First comes the healing of memories, and then comes the taking of a stand in faith to walk in today. It is not meant to say that you should live foolishly by not planning for tomorrow, but rather that you are to plan and then live in today! Be wise, plan ahead. The secret here is to plan without worry. Plan wisely, and then in faith, take any steps you need today to carry out those plans. This is a way of putting worry, or fretting, out of your life

Meditate on this and you will find there is much to be gleaned. It is a way of living one day at a time without fear of the future.

Memories are just that, memories. You are not to live in the past, but to live in the now. Ask the Lord to help you put your past in order. Ask Him to give you an understanding of how those painful memories have negatively influenced your life. Ask Him to show you how to build on the constructive memories and to dispose of the destructive ones. In that way, you open the door to a true healing of childhood memories, as well as any other memories that may cause destructive habit patterns. Remember, this is a process, but one that is worth while. It takes time, one day at a time, to bring about a total freeing.

Remember, we are not casting our past from us, but receiving a healing from destructive memories. These memories can stunt our growth in the Lord, as well as hold us in chains and bondage.

So, remember with joy, your good and constructive memories, receive a healing from your destructive memories, and you will be ready to receive all that God offers you.

> *"Therefore do not worry about tomorrow, for tomorrow will worry about itself. Each day has enough trouble of its own."* **Matthew. 6:34**
>
> *"Whenever you are arrested and brought to trial, do not worry beforehand about what to say. Just say whatever is given you at the time, for it is not you speaking, but the Holy Spirit."* **Mark 13:11**
>
> *Then Jesus said to his disciples: "Therefore I tell you, do not worry about your life, what you will eat; or about your body, what you will wear."* **Luke 12:22**
>
> *"But make up your mind not to worry beforehand how you will defend yourselves." Luke 21:14*
> *Then he adds: "Their sins and lawless acts I will remember no more."* **Hebrews. 10:17**
>
> *"Remember, therefore, what you have received and heard; obey it, and repent. But if you do not wake up, I will come like a thief, and you will not know at what time I will come to you."* **Revelation 3:3**

One Day At A Time!

Lord help me live one day
at a time,
and leave any hurtful
past behind.

Who knows if there will be
a tomorrow,
whether ahead lies joy or
sorrow.

So help me live each day
anew,
so I can walk in victory
with you!

— Betty J. Carr

FORGIVENESS

With the Holy Spirit bringing about a healing, we can function as compassionate and caring individuals. Throughout this book, there is much reference to walking in forgiveness. Again, I cannot stress enough the importance of this. This is the only way we can learn to trust again.

> *"Dear friends, do not be surprised at the painful trial you are suffering, as though something strange were happening to you. But rejoice that you participate in the sufferings of Christ, so that you may be overjoyed when His glory is revealed. If you are insulted because of the name of Christ, you are blessed, for the Spirit of glory and of God rests on you."* **1 Peter 4:12-14**

The fact that you are reading this book means that you truly desire help. The Holy Spirit is our helper. However, we have to be willing to be helped. Search your heart. Are you hurting? Have you hardened your heart? Then say the simple sinner's prayer on page 53, and you will find the pain in your heart begin to leave. When you turn to man instead of God, you will always be disappointed. God never will let you down, never forget He loves you, no matter what!

> *"Do not be overcome by evil, but overcome evil with good."* **Romans 12:21**

I suggest each morning we ask the Holy Spirit to guide and help us be more like Jesus, so that we will be able to walk in forgiveness today. Each night we should thank the Holy Spirit for helping us to heal.

We are responsible for how we act and how we perform our duties, such as being a good parent, good worker at our job, good citizen, and a good Christian role model. The joy and peace we long for can be found in Jesus. The way to Heaven is not a method or procedure that we have to work at. The way is Jesus himself, who will help us every step of the way. He has redeemed us and established a place in Heaven for all who follow Him.

"Wait for the LORD; be strong and take heart and wait for the LORD." **Psalms 27:14**

This then is the good news. We are not to lose heart. The trials and tribulations that we are going through or have gone through are temporary. The joy and the peace and glory to come are for all eternity! Whatever you have suffered, God is committed to you. Surrender to God in love and watch him bring good out of even the most seemingly unbearable situations.

"Be joyful in hope, patient in affliction, faithful in prayer." **Romans 12:12**

"The ransomed of the LORD will return. They will enter Zion with singing; everlasting joy will crown their heads. Gladness and joy will overtake them, and sorrow and sighing will flee away." **Isaiah 51:11**

SINNER'S PRAYER

If you say simply, *"Please forgive me of my sins. I believe that Jesus Christ is the Son of God, that He died for my sins; and He rose again to sit at the right hand of the Father. I invite the Holy Spirit to dwell in me and help me on the road to recovery."* He will! These are not fancy words, but, if spoken with your heart, they are all you need.

NOTES AND PRAYERS

PART SIX

OUT OF YOUR SHELL AND ON THE ROAD TO RECOVERY!

"The LORD will guide you always; he will satisfy your needs
in a sun-scorched land and will strengthen your frame.
You will be like a well-watered garden,
like a spring whose waters never fail."
Isaiah 58:11

Lonely In My Anguish

Lonely in my anguish.
Wallowing in the mire.
I failed to get my eyes off myself
and unto my Sire

Yet through my torment
You made a stand.
You looked at me and
held out Your hand.

Leading me from darkness to light,
I thank you, Lord, with all my might.
I praise, worship, love You and pray
I am now ready for You to be The Potter
with me, the clay.

— Betty J. Carr

WHAT HAVE WE LEARNED?

We have read that God loves us no matter what! We have learned how to turn the wrong messages around. We have also learned that we have choices and that we do not have to listen to, or accept negative abuse. We have learned to manage our memories. We have learned how to make an important decision the Godly way. We have also renewed our vow and commitment to Jesus Christ.

We are now ready to walk the road of recovery!

> *"My soul is weary with sorrow; strengthen me according to your word."* **Psalms 119:28**

Since we are ready to open our hearts to loved ones, friends, strangers, and more importantly, the Holy Spirit, we can now become involved in a group by volunteering in an area of expertise in our lives. You see, the best way to get over heartbreak and wounds is by helping others.

> *"Being strengthened with all power according to His glorious might so that you may have great endurance and patience, and joyfully giving thanks to the Father, who has qualified you to share in the inheritance of the saints in the kingdom of light."* **Colossians 1:11-12**

Hopeless Forlorn!

As we bustle from place to place,
we can no longer ignore a national disgrace —
a crisis of the homeless and hopeless forlorn.
They ask our help, but receive only scorn.

For them, there is no place to go;
they're without hope, and seem not to know
that the reason our dear savior was born
was for you and me, and the helpless forlorn.

But if we fed them, loved them, and showed that we care,
Christ's love would shine thru each of us there.
Christ's love, when seen by the hopeless forlorn,
may turn them around, and they could be reborn.

So, let's feed them and love them
with care and respect,
and give them Christ's love,
which they do not expect.

Then the souls of these people
can turn from despair
as they learn the old truth,
Christ has always been there.

— Betty J. Carr

HELPING OTHERS

I would like to share what happened to me in order to encourage you. After working with the needy for approximately one year, a friend gave me some cases of soap and aftershave lotion to distribute during Christmas. Little did I know what God had in mind for me. By the third Christmas, we had raised enough money for 300 sleeping bags, a McDonald's free lunch, a pair of socks, a comb, a nail file, shampoo, and soap for each person. For the men, a travel kit with aftershave lotion, razor and shaving cream; for the women, the ladies in our church had hand-knit slippers, and we gave them all these, including perfume in place of the travel kit. We were blessed, and so were they. I was becoming a healed, helpful human being.

It was that Christmas that two men came up to me with tears in their eyes saying they would now be warm that night thanks to us! I was appalled to think that in our United States of America, people could freeze. What did it matter if they were alcoholics? What did it matter if they were mentally disabled? What did it matter if they were not willing to work because of being so downtrodden? What did matter, is they were human beings and they needed help?

God touched me so profoundly through those men, that a charity called "Operation Warm-Up" was born. The Lord put on my heart how it was to be run, and then He brought me a lawyer, along with helpers, and we became an official nonprofit organization. Our goal was to see that no one would be cold. In order to do this, we would make available to all charities or churches that worked with the needy, new sleeping bags, blankets, hats, socks or gloves. As much as we would have loved to have been able to hand out these life-sustaining gifts ourselves, we felt that only by giving to the organizations that dealt with the needy, could a widely diverse area of poor be helped.

The only request we had from them was their faithfulness to enclose with each item a card that said, "This is a gift from Jesus." We had a mandate though! It was this: Anyone who picked up sleeping bags and/or blankets from us had to give us a list of those they gave them to! If we did not get a list, we called them and told them they would no longer be able to receive any items from us. This was done in order to discourage pilfering or anyone receiving two items. It was positively amazing to see how all the organizations worked with us. We felt that we were not to give Bibles or tracts with these gifts because many of these people had been fed Jesus without love. We wanted this to be a gift of unconditional love.

The only way I knew how to raise money was with a golf tournament. I was a golfer and knew many influential people in the area. Our first tournament was scheduled and $14,000 was raised. Meanwhile, the Lord gave us a connection in Taiwan and we bought brand new sleeping bags for $9.00 each. Then another miracle happened. Through a very strange set of telephone calls, I was put in touch with a blanket company who made new recycled blankets, good and warm for $2.00 each. So the first year, we found ourselves with 1,000 sleeping bags, 1,000 blankets, and 1,000 pairs of socks. I had all these items stored in a big double garage and the overflow at my house.

God again worked a miracle, bringing in a man who gave us the use of a warehouse. Not one of us accepted a salary. I worked for a total of 14 years with the homeless and 10 years with Operation Warm-Up. However, it was becoming too much of a burden. I realized that God had used me as a catalyst in order for Operation Warm-up to become a nationwide service. We needed new people at the helm. By this time, my husband had left me and I was going to leave the area for further complete healing. I prayed heavily and felt compelled by the Lord to turn over Operation Warm-Up to the Ventura Rescue Mission. They have since changed the name to "Operation Work" and have received a large grant to build a school, teaching the homeless and needy a trade that will enable them to build a life for themselves and their families.

> *"And we know that in all things God works for the good of those who love Him, who have been called according to His purpose. For those God foreknew He also predestined to be conformed to the likeness of his Son, that he might be the firstborn among many brothers."* **Romans 8:28-29**

I want you to realize that all it took was an obedient, hurting servant. The benefit I have received has been immeasurable. I walk in self-esteem, although I have to battle the old feelings at times. I have a new husband who adores me. I am now a minister of the gospel, have written a book called, "The Wisdom of His Word," and this book, "You Are Loved No Matter What!" Who would have thought it? What could God have in store for you? How many people can you help?

> *"Because those who are led by the Spirit of God are sons of God."* **Romans 8:14**

> *"Be strong and take heart, all you who hope in the LORD."* **Psalms 31:24**

WHAT DOES IT TAKE?

All it takes is the knowledge that you are loved no matter what.

> *"I love those who love Me, and those who seek Me find Me."* **Proverbs 8:17**

If you can get that in your spirit and hold on to the scripture that "if God is for you, who is against you?", you have the tools. The tools in overcoming, the tools to live a healthy, productive and Holy Spirit filled life.

Remember these simple rules:

1. Turn to the Lord, and give Him the pain!
2. Be willing to let go of past hurts and forgive!
3. Ask the Holy Spirit to let you understand and truly know how much you are loved!
4. Ask for God's guidance in decisions!
5. Learn to let go!

> *"The LORD will guide you always; he will satisfy your needs in a sun-scorched land and will strengthen your frame. You will be like a well-watered garden, like a spring whose waters never fail."* **Isaiah 58:11**

> *"He gives strength to the weary and increases the power of the weak. Even youths grow tired and weary, and young men stumble and fall; but those who hope in the LORD will renew their strength. They will soar on wings like eagles; they will run and not grow weary, they will walk and not be faint."* **Isaiah 40:29-31**

GOD'S LOVE

No matter what pain you have endured, what disappointments you have met or how unloved you have felt, the answer is in Jesus and His love. He loved you so much He died for you, for without that love there would have been no shedding of His blood.

I have found that if I focus on His love, I can overcome fear, anxiety, and feeling less than — and so can you!

> *"As the Father has loved me, so have I loved you. Now remain in my love."* **John 15:9**

His love is so powerful that it brings healing to the weary soul.

Don't give up, but press on and look to our Lord and His great love for you. In that way you can embark on your very own road to recovery. The road to being whole. Take one day at a time and know as you walk each step of the way: God loves you and so do I! No matter what!

NOTES AND PRAYERS